MAPPING THE INVISIBLE: THE INFORMAL FOOD ECONOMY OF CAPE TOWN, SOUTH AFRICA

JANE BATTERSBY, MAYA MARSHAK
AND NCEDO MNGQIBISA

SERIES EDITOR: PROF. JONATHAN CRUSH

ACKNOWLEDGEMENTS

The research for this report was funded by the Canadian Government through the UPCD Tier One Program. This report has also been distributed for discussion as a Hungry Cities Partnership (HCP) Discussion Paper, www.hungrycities.net

AFSUN

Published by the African Food Security Urban Network (AFSUN)
African Centre for Cities, University of Cape Town, Private Bag X3
Rondebosch 7701, South Africa and Balsillie School of International
Affairs, Waterloo, Canada
www.afsun.org

First published 2016

ISBN 978-1-920597-20-7

Cover photo: Informal street traders at Wynberg taxi rank in Cape Town.
World Bank Photo Collection, flickr.com.

Production by Bronwen Dachs Muller, Cape Town

Printed by Print on Demand, Cape Town

AUTHORS

Jane Battersby is a senior researcher at the African Centre for Cities, University of Cape Town, South Africa

Maya Marshak is in the Environmental and Geographical Science Department, University of Cape Town

Ncedo Mngqibisa is an independent researcher

Previous Publications in the AFSUN Series

CONTENTS

TABLE

FIGURES

1. Introduction

The informal sector remains an important component of the South African food system, despite the rapid transformation and consolidation of the formal food sector since the end of apartheid. (Greenberg 2010, Ramabulana 2011, Vink and van Rooyen 2009). The Marketing of Agricultural Products Act (Act 47 of 1996) and the 2001 Strategic Plan for Agriculture were powerful tools of deregulation and liberalization within the food system. Although these policy instruments were intended to provide greater equality within the agricultural sector, they appear to have had the opposite effect. The number of commercial farming units in South Africa declined by 76% between 1990 and 2008 (Vink and van Rooyen 2009). This was part of a process of consolidation in the agricultural sector, with an increase in the number of very large agribusiness farms and a decline in mid-sized farms.

Another central feature of this transformation is in the food retail sector which is increasingly dominated by major supermarket chains (Crush and Frayne 2011). In 2003, the supermarket sector in South Africa accounted for 50-60% of all food retail, but just 2% of all food retail outlets (Weatherspoon and Reardon 2003: 337). By 2010, it accounted for 68% of all food retail, with the four largest retailers accounting for 97% of food sold within the formal retail sector (Planting 2010). The two largest supermarket chains are Shoprite Checkers (with a 38% market share) and Pick n Pay (with 31%) (GAIN 2012). In 2013, Shoprite stated that they intended to open 124 new stores in South Africa between August 2013 and June 2014 while Pick n Pay planned to open 225 new stores in the 18 months following October 2012 (Magwaza 2013, Moneyweb 2013).

In the City of Cape Town, the total number of stores owned by Shoprite Checkers in 1994 was 38, a figure that had more than doubled to 82 by 2012. Supermarkets are not only growing in number and market share but through the development of new store formats to increase their market share in their traditional middle and upper income markets. An example is Pick n Pay's partnership with BP through which they intend to build 120 new convenience stores at petrol station forecourts (Mantshantsha 2013). Supermarkets are also expanding out of their traditional middle and upper income locations into lower income areas in major urban centres, small towns and rural parts of the country (Battersby and Peyton 2014, D'Haese and Van Huylenbroeck 2005, Peyton et al 2015).

One of the leading supermarket chains has stated that it now procures 80% of its fresh produce from just ten agribusinesses (Pienaar 2011).

Efforts to incorporate smallholders into supermarket supply chains have been largely unsuccessful (van der Heijden and Vink 2013). There is also increased vertical integration within the food system, with large companies (both supermarkets and large processors) controlling all aspects of the food value chain. Farmers are increasingly tied to direct contracts with supermarkets or processors and are unable to sell their crops to alternative market sources. The ten largest packaged food companies now account for 52% of all packaged food sales in South Africa (Igumbor et al, 2012: 2).

While recent government policies and programmes – such as the Department of Trade and Industry's Industrial Policy Action Plan and the Department of Agriculture's Agro-Processing Strategy – have sought to increase the participation of small and medium agro-processors in agro-food value chains, there is little evidence to suggest that they will be successful in the absence of stronger regulation of the system as a whole. The Competition Commission reflected on the negative impact of the liberalization of the agricultural value chain as follows:

> The far-reaching liberalisation has not yielded the desired policy outcomes, in that the agricultural value chain appears to be still largely characterised by anti-competitive outcomes, including high concentration, high barriers to entry, concentration of ownership, vertical integration, as well as anti-competitive behaviour in the pricing of food. These have serious consequences for the welfare of the poorest households given the importance of key staple foodstuffs in South Africa. Further, the highly concentrated and vertically integrated market structures of the industry may ultimately hinder constructive responses to a more developmental state approach including increasing participation in the sector (Competition Commission 2008: 4).

While formal agri-business has come to dominate the production, processing, retailing and marketing of food, the informal food retail economy has shown considerable resilience. Although supermarkets account for the greater proportion of food sales in the country, they remain a tiny minority of all food retail outlets, the vast majority of which operate in the informal food economy. Although there are no reliable figures for the number of informal food retailers in South Africa, some estimates put the number at around 100,000 spazas (informal convenience stores in residential neighbourhoods) and 750,000 *spazas* plus street traders combined (Coetzer and Pascarel 2014).

Retail is an important component of the informal sector in general, accounting for around 46% of all employment within the sector (Stats SA 2012). Around 40% of retail sales (excluding transport equipment,

household fuel and power) are channelled through informal markets (Woodward et al 2011). The informal sector contributes between 8% and 10% of South Africa's GDP. The existing evidence suggests that informal retail is dominated by the food trade (Skinner and Haysom 2016). Using third quarter 2014 QLFS data, Rogan and Skinner 2017: 13) estimate 67% of street traders sell food and the food retail sector accounts for around 30% of national food retail sales. In some food categories, including staple vegetables with a long shelf life, informal retail commands an even bigger market share.

While the informal food economy is often viewed as separate from the formal food system, and under serious threat from its expansion, it does connect to the formal economy in many ways. These include the sourcing of food from major processors, from municipal fresh produce markets, and from wholesalers. Potatoes South Africa, for example, estimates that informal traders purchase 53% of all potatoes sold at fresh produce markets (DAFF 2012). The question is whether the informal food trade will continue to grow as more supermarkets open in lower-income areas. One study estimated that between 2003 and 2005 the turnover of spaza shops in some areas was reduced by more than 20% because of the encroachment of supermarkets (van der Heijden and Vink 2013: 10). The South African Spaza and Tuckshop Association has claimed that Soweto in Johannesburg lost 30% of its spazas between 2005 and 2014 as supermarkets entered the area (Dolan 2014). Initial findings from a Demacon Market Studies survey on the impact of Jabulani Mall in Soweto were less conclusive, with 76% of informal vendors and retailers reporting no change, although the weighted percentage spend at local vendors dropped from 25% to 14% (McGaffin 2010). Another study found that the impact on small vendors of a mall development was generally negative and that those who survived did so by changing their business model (Ligthelm 2008).

This report argues that it is essential to understand the dynamics of the informal food retail sector because of its vital role in ensuring greater access to food by the urban poor. Existing policy frameworks to address food security and to govern the informal sector tend to neglect informal retail in the food system. As a result, the sector is poorly understood. The report therefore attempts to identify the characteristics of the sector that impact on its ability to address the food needs of the neighbourhoods in which the businesses are located. Although the research is focused on Cape Town, the findings are of broader relevance.

2. METHODOLOGY

This report is based on two sources of data: (a) a household food security baseline survey conducted by AFSUN in 2008 in Cape Town and (b) fieldwork conducted in Philippi and Khayelitsha during July and August 2013 that included a mapping and survey of food vendors. In the AFSUN survey, 1,060 households were interviewed in three low-income neighbourhoods of the city: Ocean View, Philippi (Ward 34) and Khayelitsha (Ward 95). According to Census 2011, 78% of the households in Ward 34 and 79% of the households in Ward 95 had incomes of less than ZAR3,200 per month. The survey included questions on the food-sourcing strategies of households, which provide insights on the relative importance of the informal food economy and other retail sources, including supermarkets (Battersby 2011a). Levels of household food insecurity were measured using the Household Food Insecurity Access Scale (HFIAS) and the Household Food Insecurity Prevalence (HFIAP) typology (Coates et al 2007).

To generate a spatial representation of the nature and distribution of informal food retail within the two sites, the research team conducted a mapping exercise using GPS units and a basic survey tool. Current ward maps overlaid on aerial photographs were obtained from the City of Cape Town's City Maps and Spatial Data Department. The wards were then divided into walkable units and small fieldwork teams of two or three people were set up to map each unit. Each team was issued with a GPS unit and a short questionnaire that captured time of interview, georeference, types of food being sold, and basic information about the business. The teams then captured the location of each informal food retail outlet they encountered on the GPS unit and filled in corresponding details on the questionnaire paper. The data was extracted from the GPS units after each day of fieldwork and then mapped and entered into an excel spreadsheet. After the spatial data had been collected, the outlets were classified according to the main food type sold and these were mapped.

The second phase of the 2013 research involved a return to the mapped areas and administering longer questionnaires to a sub-sample of the mapped vendors. In this phase, 100 questionnaires were administered with the sample determined by the proportion of vendors falling into a particular retail type (including main product traded and location relative to busy roads). The longer questionnaire addressed issues including retailer characteristics, locational strategy, business practices, sourcing of retail products and problems experienced by vendors. Finally, open-

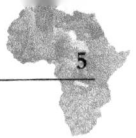

ended interviews were conducted with 15 traders and businesses supplying vendors and consumers.

In total, the study mapped 492 food traders operating in Wards 34 and 95. However, it is by no means certain that the methodology captured all traders in these urban spaces. The research team was advised not to conduct research on the weekends because of safety concerns. However, some informal food vendors, particularly those operating braai (cooked meat/barbeque) stands and selling livestock, operate only on weekends. In the mapping phase, a number of vendors were omitted, mostly Somali-owned *spaza* stores. The operators were generally not the owners of the stores and would not speak without the owner's permission. In addition, xenophobic attacks on Somali *spaza* shops have made refugees and other immigrants extremely wary of divulging information (Gastrow and Amit 2015). It was also difficult to obtain reliable data on incomes and expenditures of food vendors. Many vendors had heard rumours that the City planned to tax informal vendors and were hesitant to share financial details.

3. Informal Food and Household Food Security

The AFSUN survey found that poor households in Cape Town purchase food from three main sources: supermarkets, small formal retail outlets (such as corner shops, grocers, butchers and fast-food outlets) and informal retailers. In the year prior to the survey, 94% of the households had purchased food at supermarkets, 75% at small retail outlets and 66% from informal vendors (Figure 1). However, this underestimates the importance of the informal food economy.

Although more households purchase food at supermarkets, the majority of households only patronize supermarkets once a month, which could be a function of lack of accessibility or because supermarkets are used to purchase certain kinds of staple items in bulk or because households only have sufficient disposable income to patronize supermarkets on pay-days (Battersby 2011). Most households purchasing food from informal vendors do so on a weekly or daily basis, which is partly a reflection of their accessibility but also because they sell foodstuffs in smaller, more affordable quantities (Figure 1). Many also allow their customers to buy on credit (see below).

FIGURE 1: Sources of Food in Low-Income Areas of Cape Town

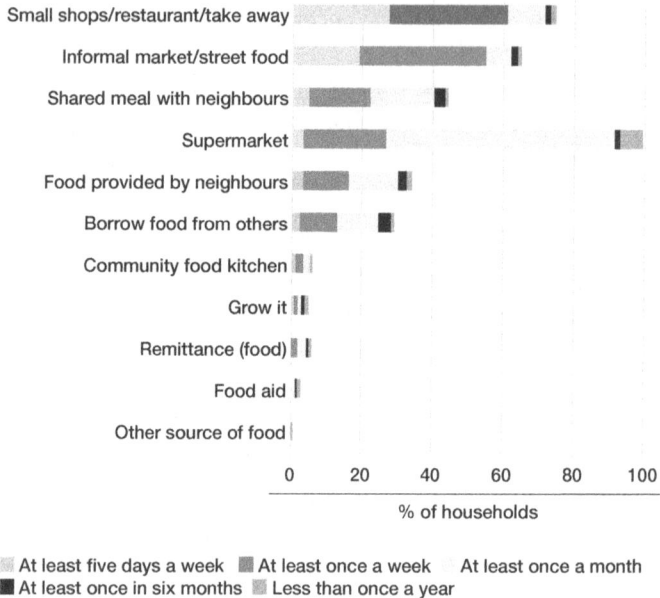

Small shops/restaurant/take away
Informal market/street food
Shared meal with neighbours
Supermarket
Food provided by neighbours
Borrow food from others
Community food kitchen
Grow it
Remittance (food)
Food aid
Other source of food

0   20   40   60   80   100

% of households

At least five days a week   At least once a week   At least once a month
At least once in six months   Less than once a year

There proved to be marked differences in the food-sourcing strategies of food-secure and food-insecure households within the three low-income neighbourhoods of the city (Figure 2). Using the HFIAP typology, all households were allocated to one of two categories: food insecure (severely food insecure/moderately food insecure) and food secure (mildly food insecure/food secure). Food-insecure households were less likely to source food from supermarkets than their food-secure neighbours and to patronize them less frequently. The proportion of food-secure households that shopped at supermarkets on a weekly basis was significantly higher than that of food-insecure households.

A similar proportion of food-secure and food-insecure households patronized informal vendors, but the food insecure tended to source their food this way more frequently. This is the result of their lower income levels that make it difficult for them to buy food in the unit sizes offered by supermarkets. Additionally, lack of income stability shapes purchasing patterns. In her work in Manenberg, for example, Cooke (2012: 95) found that four out of five households that bought food daily and depended on informal food retailers had a household member engaged in temporary or casual labour.

The expansion of supermarkets into African cities has been termed a potential "urban food security boon" because of the ability of supermarkets to lower food prices (Reardon and Minten 2011). However, Figure 2 indicates that for most food-insecure consumers, the informal food economy is the daily food source of choice. The physical presence

of supermarkets does not in itself make them accessible to the most food insecure. The retail model practised by the informal sector makes food much more accessible to those most vulnerable to food insecurity (Table 1). The informal food retail sector therefore plays an important role in the food security of the urban poor. It is particularly well aligned to households with extremely limited incomes only able to buy in small unit sizes, and often on credit. It is also well suited to the needs of households with limited refrigeration and storage capacity.

FIGURE 2: Sources of Food by Level of Food Insecurity in Low-Income Areas of Cape Town

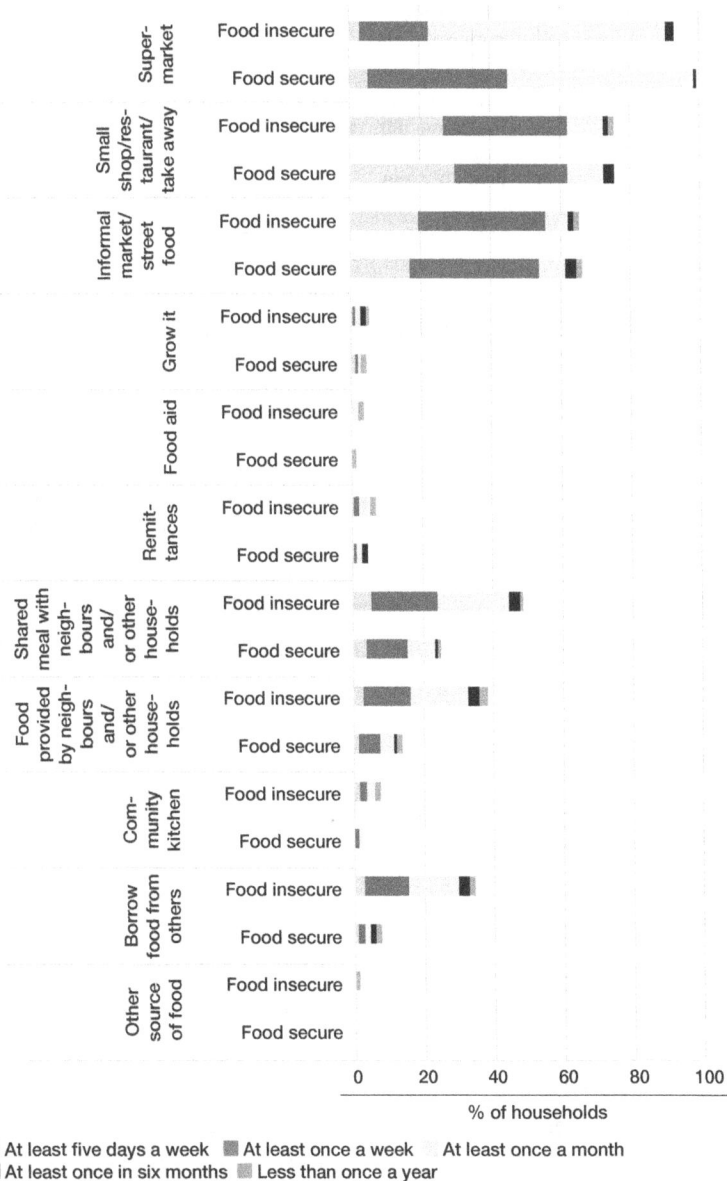

At least five days a week   At least once a week   At least once a month
At least once in six months   Less than once a year

TABLE 1: Comparison of Different Forms of Food Retail		
	Advantages	Disadvantages
Supermarkets	1. Lower prices per unit 2. Higher safety standards 3. Large range of foods	1. Unit sizes unaffordable for poorest 2. Inconvenient locations 3. Limited opening hours 4. No credit offered
Spazas	1. Affordable unit sizes for the poor 2. Sale of food on credit 3. Long opening hours 4. Convenient locations	1. Costs more than super markets per unit weight 2. Perceived low quality of food 3. Limited range of foods
Fresh produce vendors	1. Convenient location for daily purchase 2. Produce restocked daily 3. Often cheaper than supermarkets	1. Limited shelf life of produce due to lack of cold chain
Meat vendors and livestock vendors	1. Cultural preferences 2. Range of cuts of meat, including "fifth quarter" 3. Argued to taste better (live chicken)	1. Food safety
Note: This table is based on the findings presented in this report		

4. THE INFORMAL RETAIL ENVIRONMENT

Informal food retail has sometimes been characterized as more expensive, and lower in quality and range, than formal retail outlets (Tustin and Strydom 2006). It has also been seen as a marginal economic activity dominated by survivalists (Preisendörfer et al 2012). The following sections of this report seek to challenge these assumptions and to demonstrate the diversity within the informal food retail sector. The discussion first focuses on the geography and main types of food trading, and is followed by an analysis of the characteristics of the vendors themselves. This is followed by a discussion of trading practices and their responsiveness to consumer needs, a brief discussion of the reported impact of supermarkets on vendors, and the problems experienced by food vendors.

Figures 3 and 4 present the findings of the mapping exercise in Ward 34 in Philippi and Ward 95 in Khayelitsha. Almost 80% of the vendors mapped were either general dealers/*spazas* (39%), meat vendors (20%) or fruit and vegetable vendors (19%). The rest were vendors of prepared (cooked) food, livestock sellers (mainly chickens) and what were characterized as "other" (such as vendors selling some food alongside other products as their main business, or selling only sweets and chips). The total number of meat vendors (braaied meat stands) and livestock vendors was probably an under-count given the fluidity of their trading practices and, as noted above, the absence of weekend data collection.

The mapping exercise revealed the existence of distinct geographies of informal trade. In Ward 34, there was dense food retail around the train station (at the bottom of Figure 3) and along the road from the station leading up to Sheffield Road. The trade in this area is dominated by small-scale braaied meat stands and sellers of takeaway foods such as *vetkoek* (dough deepfried in oil). The road itself is a major thoroughfare for people using trains and minibus taxis to and from work. The busiest times of the day coincide with commuting peaks. Meat vendors near the station tend to sell cheaper cuts, such as offal and chicken feet. There is also significant trading and cooking of meat, including pork steaks, along New Eisleben Road. People come from other areas to Philippi to buy meat there, and these operations are also larger than those near the station.

Spaza shops tend to be scattered throughout the ward, since they serve very local populations. There are also clusters of fruit and vegetable retailers directly outside the shopping mall on the corner of New Eisleben and Lansdowne roads. Their presence is a response to the limited range and quality of produce stocked by the supermarket in the mall.

FIGURE 3: Spatial Distribution of Informal Food Vendors in Ward 34, Philippi

In Ward 95, there is dense food retail at the busy intersection of Jeff Masemola Road and Nyanda Ave (top right of Figure 4). This intersection is a junction point for minibus taxis. About 400 metres further west along

Jeff Masemola Road is a shopping mall with a Shoprite supermarket. As in Ward 34, a cluster of informal traders operates outside this mall. This ward has two train stations, but they did not have the same kind of clustering observed in Ward 34. This may be because the train stations are recent developments and their design, and that of the surrounding areas, may preclude the density of trade evident in Ward 34. Additionally, in this area of Khayelitsha informal minibus taxis have been banned. This may serve to make the station a less viable site for traders.

FIGURE 4: Distribution of Informal Food Vendors in Ward 95, Khayelitsha

Within Ward 95 there is a greater density of *spaza* stores and other traders in the informal housing area than in the newly built formal state-provided housing. Those households living in formal housing are generally no wealthier than those in shacks, so it is important to consider what might be driving the sparseness of trading in the newly formalized areas. First, the informal areas have far more dense housing and therefore a potentially larger customer base. Second, the design of the state-provided housing may inhibit the establishment of informal food businesses. And finally, the residents of formal housing may have better storage facilities than those in shacks and may therefore be able to buy more in bulk and be less dependent on daily food purchases from *spazas*.

Given the small size of most of the informal food businesses, it is not surprising that just over three quarters (76%) are owner-operated. A further 16% were owned by another family member. Only 3% were owned by non-family members (3%) or collectively owned as part of a *stokvel* (or co-op) (5%). Despite the homogeneity of patterns of ownership, there is considerable diversity in the informal food sector. First, there is a clear gender difference by type of activity: participants in the general dealer/*spaza* category were predominantly male but in all other categories women outnumbered men (Figure 5). Women are more likely to be operating survivalist, micro-scale businesses. For example, multi-level, relatively permanent fruit and vegetable stands are generally operated by men, while women are more likely to be selling a few oranges and apples on an upturned box. However, women clearly dominate in meat trading, with some of the most lucrative operations in this sector.

FIGURE 5: Gender Distribution by Type of Activity

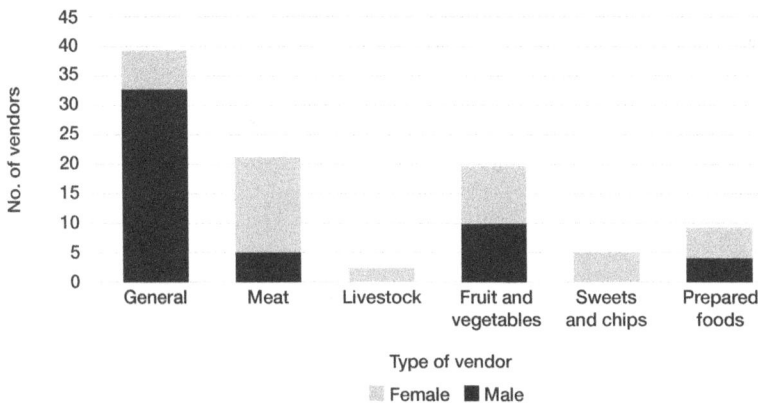

Second, the food vendors have varying levels of education (Figure 6). Only about 20% had completed secondary school and many had less schooling than that. This probably reflects the low barriers to entry in the food sector and the limited formal employment options open to residents of Wards 34 and 95. Very few have post-secondary qualifications, which suggests that educated individuals are not foregoing their qualifications and working in the informal economy. As one fruit and vegetable trader observed:

> I realised a long time ago that I'm not educated and I was already having troubles where I used to work as a construction worker. The problem was communication and I could not follow instructions very well because I never spoke or understand English or Afrikaans. I decided to open my own business. First it was the small spaza and it went to fruit and vegetables (Interview in Philippi, 29 July 2013).

Third, there was some diversity in the national origins of food vendors. One of the dominant narratives in the South African media and officialdom is that Somali vendors are driving South Africans out of business (Basadien at al 2014, Charman et al 2012, Economist 2014). Although

Somalis are generally denigrated as "foreigners" stealing from South Africans in this narrative, most are in fact refugees and have the same legal right as citizens to pursue an economic livelihood in the country. The extent of the Somali refugee presence within these two wards was not immediately apparent, as a number of Somali-owned businesses had Xhosa names. These were generally bought from South Africans and the names were retained to maintain continuity and a degree of anonymity, an important consideration in the context of the xenophobic violence that periodically flares up in Cape Town's townships (Gastrow and Amit 2015). In many cases, the former owners rent the business property to Somalis, finding landlordism more lucrative than running a business. This study found that the Somali refugee presence in the food sector is confined to only one activity: the operation of *spaza* shops (Figure 7). All other informal food sector activities are the domain of South Africans.

FIGURE 6: Educational Level of Informal Food Vendors

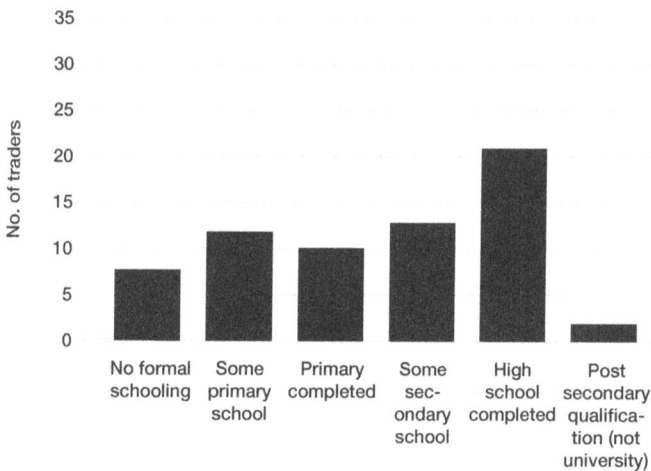

By far the most common reason given for trading in a particular location was proximity to passing customers. With the exception of the meat vendors on New Eisleben Road in Ward 35, the food vendors do not specialize to the extent that customers travel to patronize their businesses. Much of the business could be characterized as convenience shopping – buying food on the way to or from work. As a result, vendors cluster on roads with a lot of foot traffic to capture passing trade. Only a few identified proximity to a supermarket as a reason for their business location. In Manenburg, Cooke (2012) found that the location of *spazas* is determined more by proximity to the place of residence of the owner.

Most residents of Wards 34 and 95 do patronize supermarkets, but relatively infrequently. Supermarkets may therefore generate less passing trade than walking routes to train stations, for example. Supermarkets tend to be at intersections of roads with heavy road traffic, but not necessarily heavy foot traffic and so informal vendors and supermarkets have different locational strategies to maximize their different customer bases. The small number of fruit and vegetable traders outside supermarkets are generally targeting their customers by capitalizing on the deficiencies in the supermarkets' fresh produce offerings.

FIGURE 7: Country of Origin of Informal Food Vendors

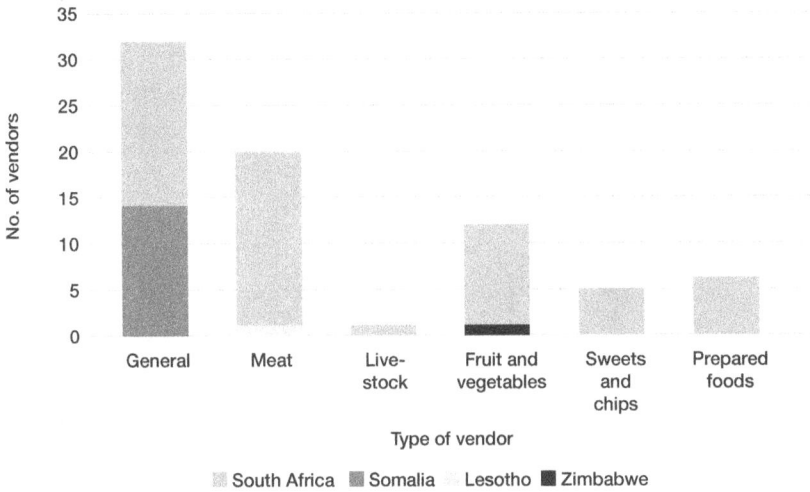

FIGURE 8: Reasons for Choosing Business Locations

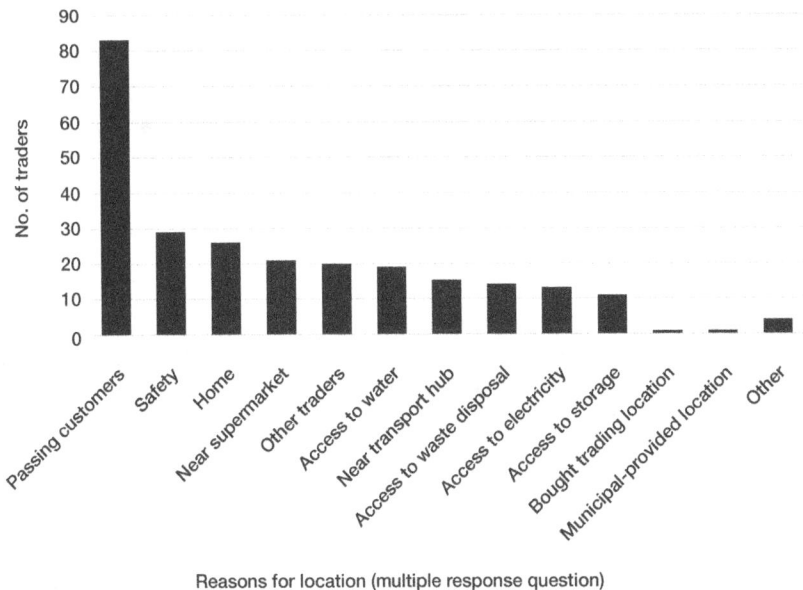

Reasons for location (multiple response question)

Safety concerns are another important determinant of location. Food vendors identified theft and vandalism as ongoing problems and often clustered together to protect their businesses. The vendors also noted that they did not want to be the last ones in the immediate area to close their business in the evening, as this left them vulnerable to crime. *Spaza* shops tend to be more isolated and vulnerable and to remain open for longer hours than other retailers, so owners take measures to protect themselves including sleeping on the premises and using old shipping containers as shops. The lack of adequate, safe storage space has been identified as a problem by trader associations in Cape Town (Bamu and Theron 2012). Over half (57%) of the respondents keep their goods at home, and a quarter at the trading location (primarily *spazas*) (Figure 9). Only 9% rent space to store their goods.

FIGURE 9: Storage Locations for Retail Goods

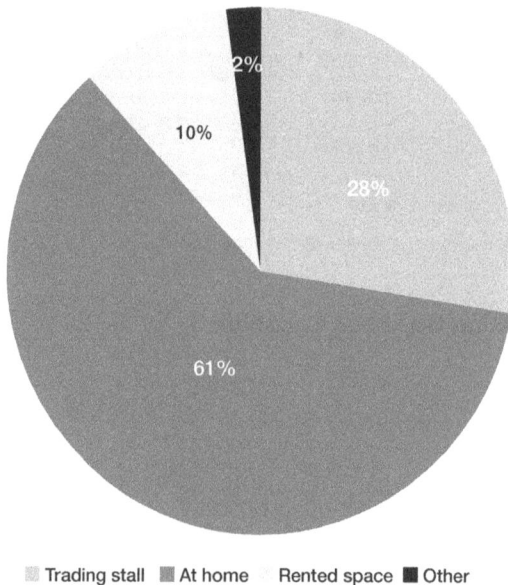

Informal food businesses are largely run by local residents (South African or foreign) and serve the local community. Most (55%), typically the *spaza* owners, live on site. Another 31% live within walking distance and just 15% come in from another part of the city. These figures provide further confirmation of the locality-based nature of informal food retail. The "localness" of informal food retail generates a form of community embeddedness that means that the stores need to be responsive to local needs and purchasing capacities in order to survive (Cooke 2012).

5. Business Strategies of Informal Food Vendors

5.1 Trading Hours

One of the reasons that the informal food retail sector is more responsive to the food security needs of the urban poor is its longer trading hours. Supermarkets rarely open before 8am and most are closed by 6pm. Given the long commuting times of many residents of Wards 34 and 95, these hours are inconvenient. Informal vendors operate longer hours to maximize their trading potential and thus serve the needs of local residents more effectively than the supermarkets. Figure 10 indicates the times of day that the vendors identified as their busiest. Trading activities peak during morning and evening commuting times and in the evenings when people are home. Vendors identified Fridays and weekends as their busiest trading days (Figure 11). A number of traders only operate on these days. This pattern is a response to the weekly pay cycle of many residents and the cultural norm of social eating on the weekends.

FIGURE 10: Busiest Trading Times for Informal Traders

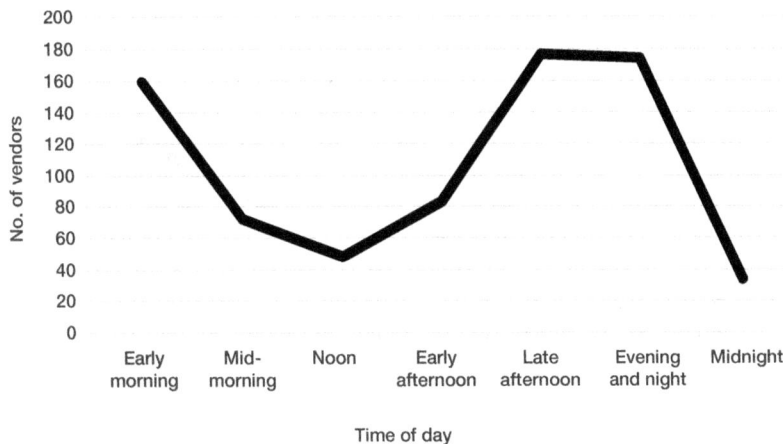

Note: Multiple response question

Over the course of a year, there are distinct highs and lows in patronage of informal vendors (Figure 12). Previous research on the temporal dimensions of food insecurity in Cape Town identified an annual pattern of high food insecurity in January (after the festive season) and during the winter months (Battersby 2011a). The most food-secure month was December. The reduction in the number of vendors in January and the high numbers in the final months of the year are consistent with the annual income and expenditure patterns identified in the earlier study. However, the rise in business activity in June and July is inconsistent with previous findings which show that this is a time of greater food insecurity for households. This might reflect increased dependence on informal food retail during the winter as households have less money to spend on food and cannot afford bulk purchasing from supermarkets. However, this is largely conjecture.

FIGURE 11: Busiest Trading Days for Informal Traders

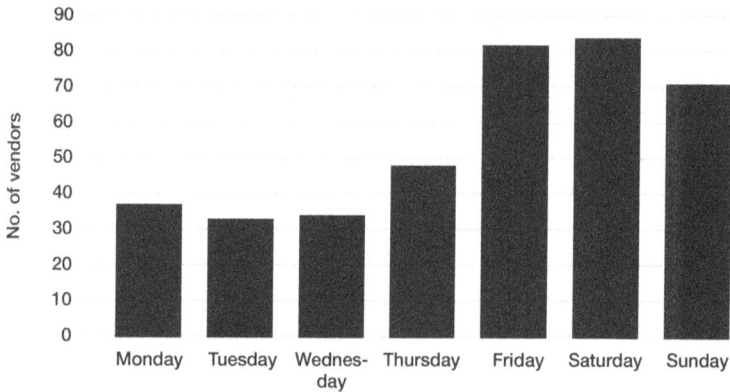

Note: Multiple response question

FIGURE 12: Busiest Trading Months for Informal Traders

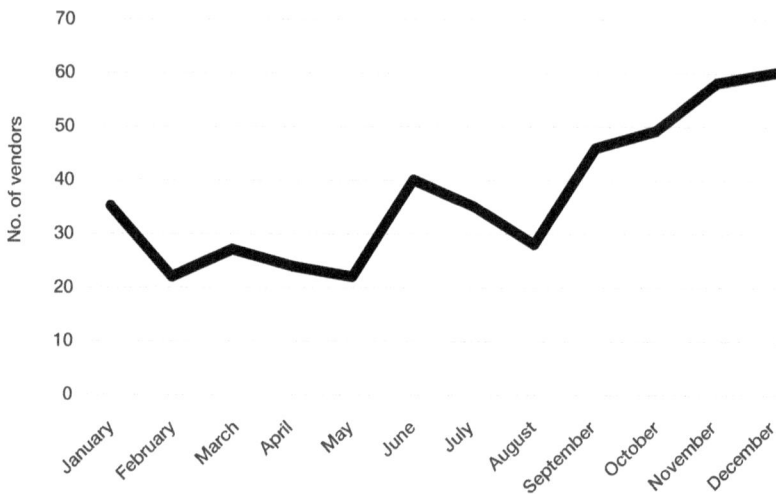

Note: Multiple response question

5.2 Sourcing Supplies

The informal food sector is closely linked to, and contributes to the profitability of, the formal food system. The sources of food utilized by the greatest number of vendors were all formal outlets: fresh produce markets, wholesalers and supermarkets (Figure 13). Most of the fresh produce sold in these low-income areas comes directly or indirectly from Cape Town Fresh Produce Market and the Golden Harvest Fresh Produce Market in Epping (www.ctmarket.co.za). These markets sell produce both to informal vendors and to major retailers such as supermarkets. The latter are guaranteed the best quality and freshest produce. Some informal vendors buy the produce in bulk and sell to others:

> There are these guys who buy in bulk and sell to the township business… They sell to other businesses. They buy many pallets. Because of that, the price significantly decreases such that they end up selling, for instance, a bag of potatoes at the same price as us inside (Interview with Golden Harvest Employee, August 2013).

FIGURE 13: Sources of Produce

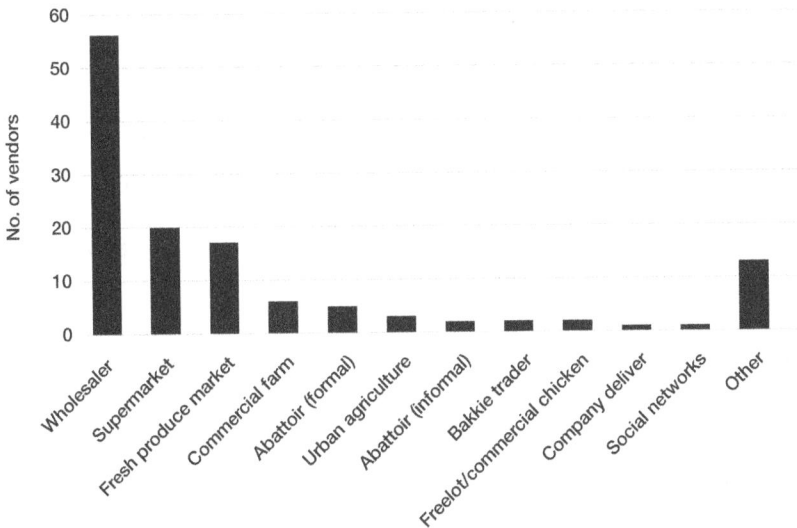

Note: Multiple response question

Vendors who buy fruit and vegetables at the Cape Town Fresh Produce Market do not always buy from the same supplier but according to price and quality on the day. This ensures that they are able to deliver the best quality produce to their customers at consistent prices. In Khayelitsha, wholesalers Mabhabhela and Metro Cash and Carry are also important sources of produce for informal vendors. Most of the fresh produce at Metro is also purchased from the Cape Town Fresh Produce Market.

Explaining why fresh produce traders buy stock from Mabhabhela, one trader noted:

> It's the cheapest and nearest market place, particularly for us without transport. You can't go to other markets because the transport is going to kill you and you may end up paying more than you would at Mabhabhela if one includes the transport fee. I take taxis and pay for a seat or two, so it's only R6 per seat because I am only occupying a space for one person. But, if I go to other markets, I will have to hire a car and they cost too much (Interview with Fruit and Vegetable Trader, Philippi, 2013).

Meat vendors access meat from local meat companies. Live chickens are sourced directly from farms. One Somali *spaza* owner said that he purchased red meat from the market in Maitland and sourced chicken from Country Fair at Epping as these were the cheapest, good quality sources.

Issues such as transportation, cash flow, storage, and lack of refrigeration determine the flows of food within the informal sector. Vendors are largely price takers, although in the case of fresh produce they are able to shop around. They cannot add much mark up as the low-income customer base cannot afford to spend more and, given the large number of vendors selling similar products in close proximity, there is intense competition.

Informal vendors make particularly frequent purchases of produce. As Figure 14 shows, most products are purchased on a weekly basis. However, milk, bread and fresh meat tend to be purchased daily as a result of limited transport, storage and refrigeration and, in the case of perishables, to ensure the freshness of the goods.

Bread and milk are generally purchased daily by consumers and vendors need to ensure that they constantly have these in stock. Fruit and vegetables also need to be restocked frequently because of spoilage. The weekly purchases of most other foodstuffs are the result of weekly trips to the wholesalers.

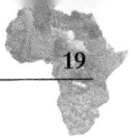

FIGURE 14: Frequency of Food Purchase by Informal Vendors

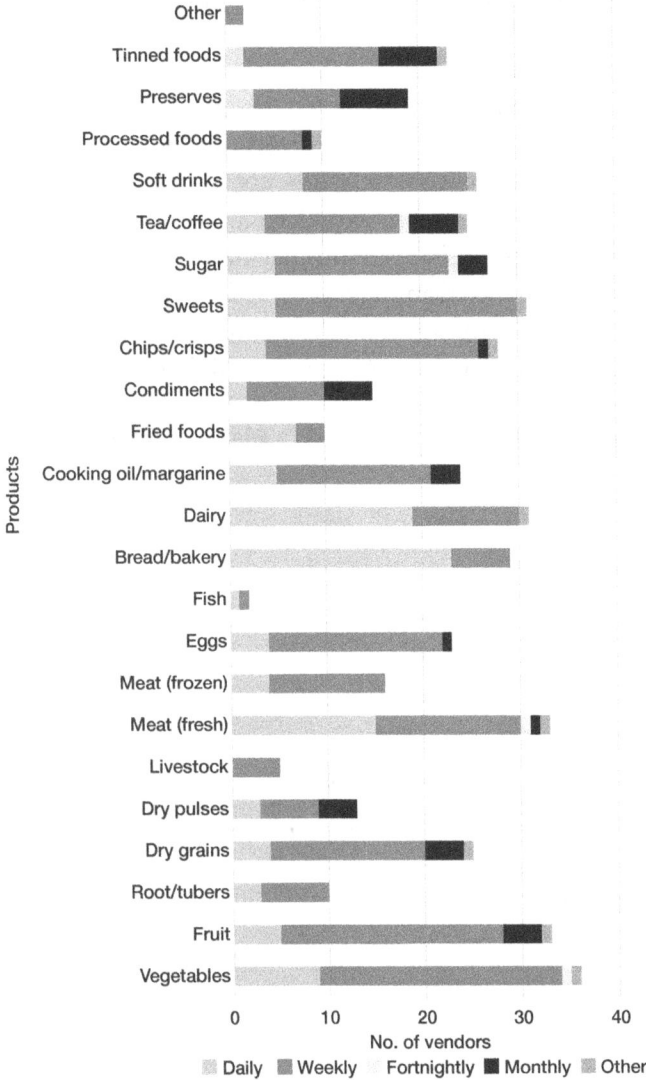

5.3 Transportation of Produce

Transportation costs play an important role in informal trade procure-
ment practices. One fruit and vegetable trader in Philippi who had his
own car spoke about his costs and charging others for transport as follows:
"People always think only about petrol when thinking about transport
money, but (there is) also your wheel treads and car maintenance." He
drives himself to the market and also takes "some of these ladies who
don't have transport" and charges them ZAR20 for petrol, and "although
that is never enough, but since I was going to the market anyway, I don't
mind that much because I am not greedy."

Figure 15 illustrates the ways in which vendors get food to their places of
retail. While there is clearly considerable diversity in methods of bringing

food to places of retail, this varies by product, scale of operation and business type. Two products tend to be delivered to *spaza* shops directly by companies: bread and soft drinks. Bread is delivered by two companies: Albany and Blue Ribbon. The vendors prefer Albany as the company takes back old bread and provides fresh bread every day. One Somali *spaza* owner in Ward 95 said that they were treated better by Albany and that the bread was cheaper. However, customers preferred Blue Ribbon bread. Although the vendors are responsive to customer needs, they do make business decisions based on upstream agents' practices. In the case of bread, Albany's practice of collecting and replacing old bread gives them an advantage in the extensive and competitive informal food retail sector.

FIGURE 15: Means of Transportation of Food to Place of Sale

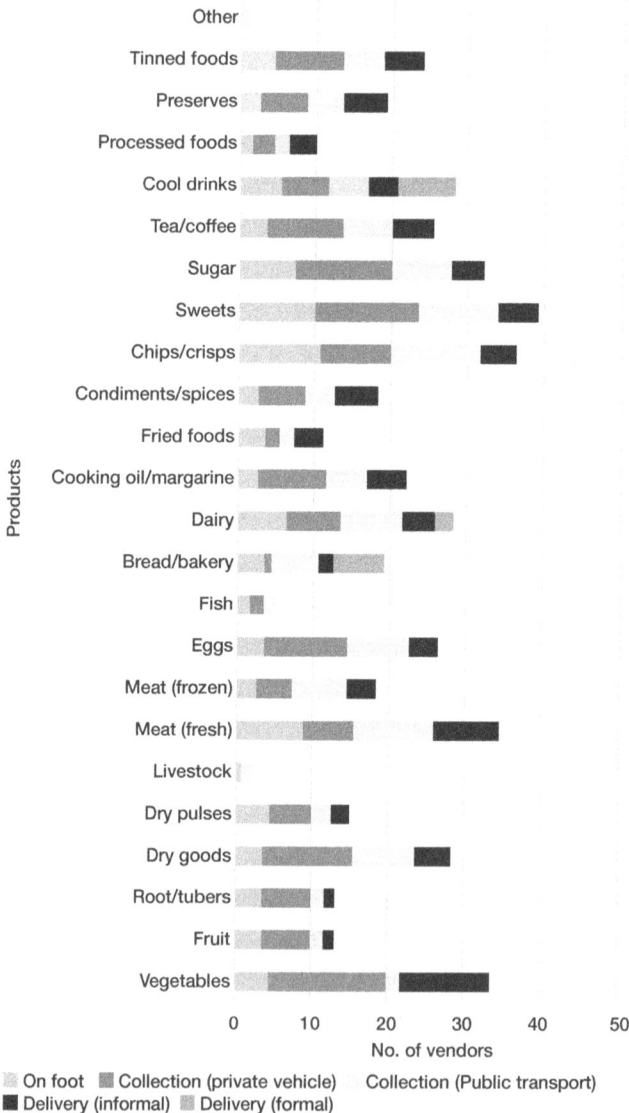

On foot   Collection (private vehicle)   Collection (Public transport)
Delivery (informal)   Delivery (formal)

5.4 Granting Credit

An important feature of the informal food retail sector that makes businesses responsive to the food security needs of their customer base is the granting of credit. Many poor households purchase food on credit when they run out of cash. Credit is important to many people in these wards who would otherwise have to obtain money from loan sharks, who charge interest rates of up to 40%. A study of the nature of indebtedness of the poor and the extent of the problem in the Cape Metropolitan Area found that many poor households are forced to borrow from money-lenders at extremely high interest rates, and that the loans are mainly used to supplement low wages for consumption purposes (Nagdee 2004). High interest rates usually lead households into a debt trap as they continuously borrow to fund their household expenditure after all their income is spent on repaying loans.

Over half (58%) of the vendors interviewed for this study offer goods on credit to customers. Eighty percent of those who provide credit do so to "known customers." The rest provide it to family members or neighbours only. Given the economically marginal nature of many of these businesses it is perhaps surprising that so many offer credit. According to Cooke (2012), the business model of the *spaza* trades off profit maximization and business sustainability:

> The willingness of [spaza] owners to provide credit is the result of recognition of both the role which their businesses play as a node in the community food network and their reliance on the support of this community for the survival of their shop. Their business practices are mediated through both a desire to create a profit and desire to build social capital, a dynamic which is not found in the formal retail sector (Cooke 2012: 134).

As many as 70% of credit-granting businesses charge no interest. This gives customers a means to access food without creating further debt, and is therefore a vital safety net for the urban poor.

Repayment rates on credit are high. This is perhaps a function of the practice of lending only to known customers. However, 18% of vendors said they were repaid only sometimes and 2% rarely or never. According to research in Manenberg, vendors continue to lend as they depend on their small local customer base, and are willing to incur some bad debt to maintain their client base and therefore their own business viability (Cooke 2012).

The need to be responsive to the local customer base is also evident in the differences in credit granting practices of the different types of informal food retailers. General stores (mainly *spazas*), for example, are more likely to offer goods on credit and less likely to charge interest (Figure 16). As noted earlier, the *spazas* tend be located within residential areas and are less likely to have casual customers. Their more localized and consistent customer base makes it in their interest to offer interest-free credit.

FIGURE 16: Credit-Granting Practices

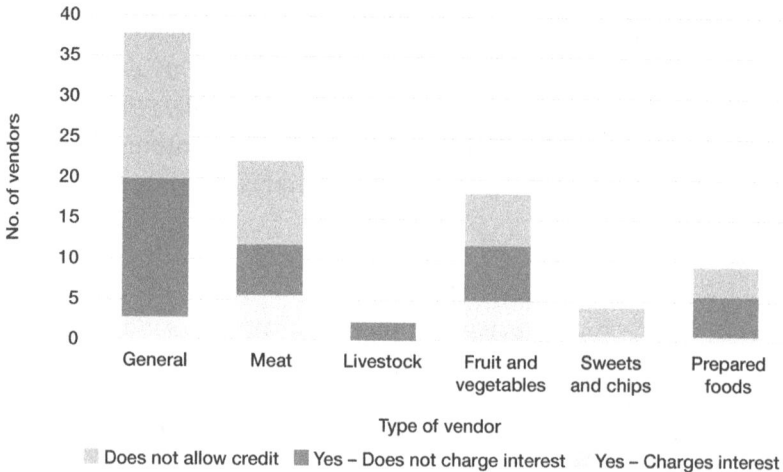

If it is acknowledged that these vendors are an essential source of food for the urban poor, then it is important to understand the barriers to their business survival. The food vendors themselves identified several problems that affect their businesses.

6. BUSINESS CHALLENGES IN THE INFORMAL FOOD ECONOMY

6.1 Competition from Supermarkets

There has been a rapid expansion of supermarkets into low-income areas in Cape Town in recent years (Battersby and Peyton 2014). Concerns have been expressed that these supermarkets will undercut informal vendors and even drive them out of business, as they have in other areas (Battersby 2011a, van der Heijden and Vink 2013). If vendors can withstand the first shock of supermarket entry and are willing to extend credit, then their businesses might recover from the impact of the opening of a supermarket. As one fresh produce vendor in Philippi noted, when asked whether a new supermarket had affected his business: "Yes and no, because when they start their prices are low but after three months they [the customers] come back to us because supermarkets don't give out credit for food." The results from the research on Cape Town suggest that the impacts of supermarkets on informal food retail are complex, with conflicting experiences of the impact of supermarkets even by traders within the same vendor type (Figure 17). Many vendors may not be in a position to assess the real impact of supermarkets given the high turnover and short lifespan of businesses. There is a high turnover of businesses in the food sector: one study has estimated that up to 50% of new entrants into the *spaza* business survive for less than five years, although those that do survive have considerable longevity (Charman et al 2012: 51). This bimodal pattern was evident in this study with 58% of the businesses in operation for 5 years or less and 18% for 10 years or more (Figure 18). Among the latter was a meat trader who had taken over the stand from her father and the business had been running for over 20 years.

FIGURE 17: Perceived Impact of Supermarkets on Informal Vendors

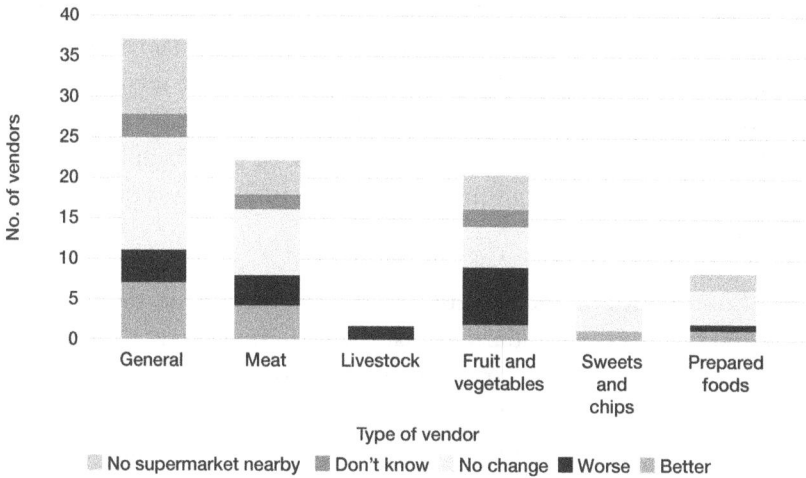

Nearly 40% indicated that there had been no change to their business and 16% said that their business had even improved with the advent of supermarkets. Only 18% said that it had declined. The perceived impact of supermarkets did vary with the type of enterprise. Fresh produce vendors were the most likely to indicate that the supermarkets had been bad for business (Figure 17). This was surprising given the clustering of fresh produce vendors outside supermarkets. A surprisingly high number of general vendors/*spazas* indicated that the presence of supermarkets had either not affected or had been good for their businesses. This may be because the presence of a supermarket nearby provides easier access for vendors to restock their supplies without incurring high transport costs.

FIGURE 18: Years of Operation of Informal Food Businesses

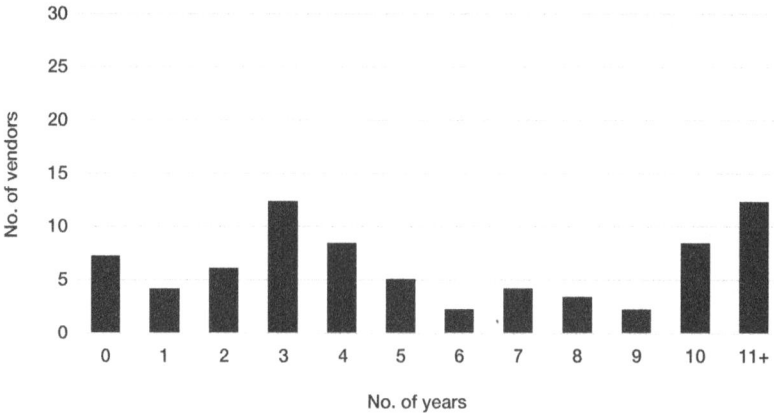

One reason why the impact of supermarkets on informal food vendors may not be as severe as anticipated is the longstanding practice of supermarket "outshopping" by residents. Outshopping is when people patronize shops and supermarkets outside their residential area. In South Africa, the practice was originally associated with the lack of formal retail within township areas, and connected to a mismatch between the retail environment and the spending power of the emerging black middle class (Strydom 2011, Tustin and Strydom 2010). In Soweto, for example, 91% of the retail spend of the most affluent households in 2004 was outshopped (Ligthelm 2008: 38).

Despite the growing presence of supermarkets in Khayelitsha, the residents interviewed for this study indicated that they continue to do their supermarket shopping outside the area, preferring supermarkets in Mitchell's Plain because of perceived better food quality. In addition, some residents employed outside the township continued to buy at supermarkets near to their place of work because of convenience, perceived superior quality and the fact that local supermarkets are closed by the time they get home. The pre-existence of outshopping may mute the impact of supermarket expansion, as many consumers able to purchase from supermarkets are already doing so, albeit in a different location.

Another reason why vendors may not feel the impact of supermarket expansion is because they are not in direct competition, initially at least. Studies in other contexts have noted that customers move slowly from purchasing from informal vendors to supermarkets on a product-by-product basis, starting with processed foods and ending with fresh produce (Reardon et al 2007: 408).

6.2 Waste Management and Pollution

One of the most common problems faced by food vendors is spoilage, identified by over half of the vendors as a challenge (Figure 19). Vendors often do not have adequate storage or refrigeration, either on-site or at home, which means that their stock has a limited shelf life. Additionally, much of the fresh produce they stock has not been part of a cold chain, having been purchased from other vendors and transported in open-topped vehicles. Likewise, the dependence of vendors on their own collection or delivery means that many of their products arrive at the point of sale damaged and overheated.

Given the high spoilage rates, it is important to understand what vendors do with spoiled or expired foods. The question of waste management is a food system and food security issue, but also a health and safety question. Research on informal vendors operating outside the Cape Town Fresh Produce Market found that much of the spoiled fresh produce was distributed to those unable to buy food (Jackson 2010). A study in Khayelitsha found that meat vendors were employing a variety of unsafe meat and meat by-product disposal strategies (Madlokazi 2011). As Figure 20 indicates, much of the spoiled or expired food is still consumed, being passed on to others as a charitable act (46%), sold at discounted prices (29%), or consumed by the vendor (24%).

FIGURE 19: Operating Problems Faced by Informal Food Vendors

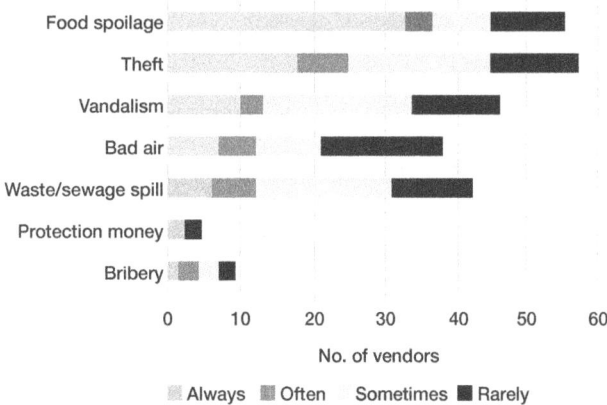

Food waste that cannot be consumed is disposed of. Some vendors take their waste to the dump and others simply use their bins at home. In areas where skips are provided by the municipality, they are used by vendors. However, the waste collection day of the week is not necessarily aligned to periods of peak waste (Madlokazi 2011). Meat vendors are particularly busy over weekends and most waste is generated then. However, waste collection is managed on an area-by-area daily rota. This may mean that the waste is not collected from the skips until Thursday, by which time it is putrid, foul smelling and dangerous.

Vendors were also concerned about environmental conditions that affected their businesses. The problem of pollution ("bad air") is particularly evident in areas with a high density of cooked meat stands. The more marginal stands use a range of materials including salvaged treated wood and even plastic as fuel. This creates toxic fumes that are unpleasant for passing customers and dangerous if inhaled. Waste and sewage spills are common in these areas and are not only unpleasant, but particularly hazardous for businesses serving food.

FIGURE 20: Strategies to Deal with Spoiled or Expired Foods

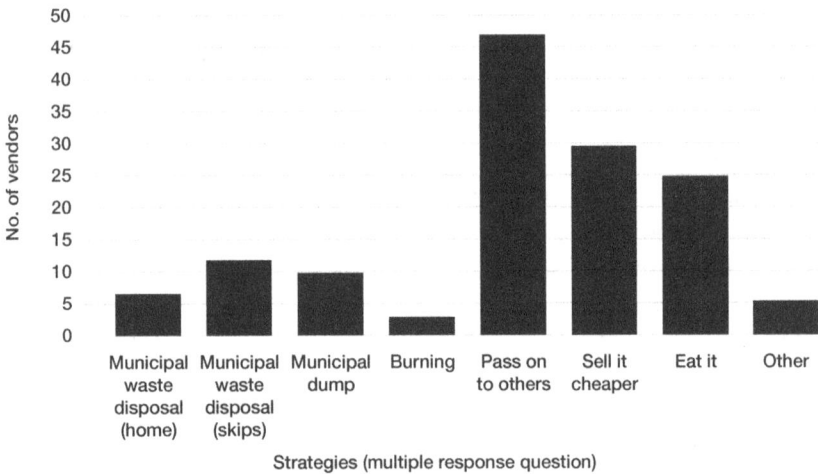

6.3 Security Challenges

Other common problems included theft and vandalism, noted by 57% and 46% of the vendors respectively. One snack seller noted that she also used to sell fruit, but "the crime rate changed all of that and I could no longer secure my stock because I lost a lot of money." The experience and fear of crime also impacts on business practices and viability, affecting the hours of trade, the location of trade and the amount of stock carried. A few vendors identified the soliciting of protection money by local gangs or bribes to law enforcement officials as problems.

7. POLICIES TOWARDS INFORMAL FOOD RETAIL

This section identifies two major policy gaps:

- The role of informal food retail as a component of food security is neglected within South African food security strategies and programmes; and

- Policy and programmes regarding the informal sector focus almost exclusively on informal retail as a livelihood and neglect its role in providing essential goods and services to the urban poor.

7.1 National Food Security Programmes

South Africa does not have a comprehensive food security policy, despite the right of access to food being recognized as a constitutional right in Section 27.1 of the Constitution. In 2002, the national government established a Food Price Monitoring Committee and an Integrated Food Security Strategy (IFSS). Despite its magnitude and importance, informal food retail is neglected in both. A major 2003 report commissioned by the government on food pricing also neglected the informal sector (FPMC 2003). While there has been significant interest and concern about food price inflation, informal retail outlets have been consistently omitted from calculations of the CPIF (the food component of the Consumer Price Index). Ten years after the omission was first flagged by the Food Price Monitoring Committee, StatsSA finally announced a revision of the basket of goods calculation to include a greater focus on price data from retailers in informal areas (Kelly 2013). However, the food items in the new basket of goods reflected only the changing purchasing habits of the rising black middle class. As a result, several staple foods of the urban poor were removed and items such as filter coffee and drinking chocolate were added. It is therefore not clear that the revised basket will provide a better analytical tool for understanding the informal food retail sector and its contribution to the food system and food security.

The IFSS's stated vision is "to attain universal physical, social and economic access to sufficient, safe and nutritious food by all South African at all times to meet their dietary and food preferences for an active and healthy life" (DoA 2002: 6). The IFSS further states that "food security policies must address all aspects of the food system, affecting the entire conceptual spectrum, ranging from production, marketing, distribution, all the way to consumption and nutrition" (DoA 2002: 6). According to the IFSS, food policy interventions require that both micro and macro issues be addressed and are designed in such a manner that they resolve issues of malnutrition and food security; involve policy and programme design and implementation that cut across departmental divisions; consider a wide array of data that can be disaggregated down to the household level (or even to the intra-household level); and deal with conflicting policy objectives that arise between producers and consumer interests, urban and rural differences, primary and secondary production, budgetary prioritization between consumption support and investment in agriculture, and short- and long-run decisions (DoA 2001: 17).

Despite these allusions to a systemic approach to food security, the strategy actually focuses primarily on providing access to productive resources (Drimie and Ruysenaar 2010). Where such resources are unavailable, it focuses on providing income and job opportunities to enable households to purchase food and, failing this, a set of social safety net responses are envisaged (DoA 2002: 6-7). These aims are at odds with the whole food system approach described elsewhere in the document, and place the focus on household-scale rather than systemic interventions. The IFSS never mentions the informal sector. It does speak about reducing vulnerability to market fluctuations and strengthening market systems, but nowhere is there any indication that the informal sector is considered part of this market.

The major food and nutrition programmes of national government – the Integrated Nutrition Programme (INP) and the National Schools Nutrition Programme – also do not have an explicit focus on food system issues. The original 1994 INP, housed within the Department of Health, included a call for community-based nutrition projects, which would encourage "multisectoral government support to communities to 'solve' their own nutrition problems" (Labadarios et al 2005: 102). Part of this approach was the inclusion of food-based income generation projects. However, the promotion of such projects was omitted from subsequent iterations of the INP as they were deemed to be unrealistic and lacked appropriate resources.

More recently, the 2012 National Development Plan has provided room for a more nuanced view of the food system as contributing to or hindering food security (NPC 2012: 39, 40, 116). For example, it speaks of the need to reduce the cost of food and calls for a stable food inflation environment. Additionally, it advocates for a policy framework that (a) responds to the bottlenecks in the food system that create food insecurity and (b) fosters investment in agriculture and agro-processing as areas of SMME

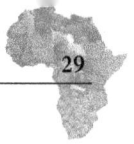

growth for job creation and to redress skewed ownership patterns (NPC 2012: 142, 289). Although there is no explicit focus here on markets and the role of informal food retail in the food system, it does provide potential entry points for further engagement. This is because it draws attention to the role of the food system in food security, and acknowledges the power imbalances within the existing system. The assertion of the need for a systemic approach (which includes a range of government departments), provides greater scope for the engagement of municipal government within food security interventions. This includes spatial planning, zoning, economic development planning, and informal trade support.

In 2014, the South African government gazetted a National Policy on Food and Nutrition Security (DAFF 2014). The policy has been criticized by civil society organizations because it "was not subject to any public consultation and is utterly deficient in its identification of problems with the food system in South Africa and its failure to come up with solutions" (Section 27: 2014). Among the deficiencies is a lack of engagement with food retail in general and the informal food retail sector in particular.

The policy defines food and nutrition security as "access to and control over the *physical, social and economic means* to ensure sufficient, safe and nutritious food at all times, for all South Africans, in order to meet the dietary requirements for a healthy life" [italics added] (DAFF 2014: 8) and claims to be built on four pillars: (a) adequate availability of food; (b) accessibility (physical, social and economic) of food; (c) utilization, quality and safety of food; and (d) stability of food supply. However, the question of access is reduced to a discussion of food prices and access to markets refers only to smallholder farmers looking to sell produce (DAFF 2014: 13-14). While there is a focus on issues of food preservation and utilization, the policy focuses only on the household and agricultural sectors as areas of attention (DAFF 2014: 15). The new policy therefore fails to address the concerns about the Integrated Food Security Strategy and does not engage the realities of the urban food system as it relates to the urban poor.

7.2 Informal Trade Policies and Programmes

The policy neglect of the role of the informal food retail sector in food security is symptomatic of a wider neglect of the informal sector as a whole (Battersby 2011b, Rogerson 2016). Despite the importance of the informal economy, there has been relatively little policy support and funding directed towards effective governance of this sector. The informal sector is generally considered only in terms of its role as a provider of livelihoods, and food vending is generally not considered as a separate category. However, food sales are an important component of informal trade. A 2012 study of Delft in Cape Town mapped 818 micro-businesses, of which 64% were selling food and/or beverages (Charman et al 2012). A similar picture emerges in other South African cities: a survey of informal street traders operating in metropolitan Durban in 2003, for example, found that 60% were selling food (Skinner 2008).

Since informal food vendors make such an important contribution to food security, informal trade needs to be reframed in policy terms to consider its contribution of essential goods and services to the wider community and not simply to those obtaining income through participation. The City of Cape Town has noted the importance of the informal sector to its economy, and has had an Informal Trading Policy and Management Framework since 2003 (CoCT 2003). In its mission statement, the framework notes that "through a developmental approach, the City seeks to facilitate the access to job and entrepreneurial opportunities in the informal trading sector and the nurturing of a positive relationship with the formal business sector by providing a stable regulatory and flexible management environment that is predictable, empowering and sustainable" (CoCT 2003: 6). The framework aims to create a "well-managed informal trading sector that is fully integrated into the economic, spatial and social development objectives of the City." The City has an informal trade management unit within its Economic Development Department and in 2013 it hosted an informal trading summit.

The City's 2013 Economic Growth Strategy recognizes the importance of the informal sector, identifying it as "a key site of entrepreneurial activity and a source of employment" (CoCT 2013a: 28). It therefore proposes that the City provide a "positive enabling role…by better coordinating its local development programmes and by introducing regulatory changes that facilitate genuine entrepreneurial activity in the informal economy" (CoCT 2013a: 28). This focus on entrepreneurialism is also present in the City's Social Development Strategy (CoCT 2013b: 3). The focus thus remains on the employment potential of the sector and the promotion of entrepreneurialism, rather than on the goods and services provided by the sector to the city's residents. However, a model to promote economic growth may not necessarily promote wider food security. With the exception of some of the meat vendors, food businesses are not highly profitable enterprises with potential for growth. Additionally, the precarity of these businesses is the very thing that ensures that they are responsive to the needs of the poorest customers, including the offering of credit and the willingness to bulk break.

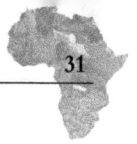

The City's 2013 Informal Trading By-Law has been roundly criticized by informal vendors and researchers who argue that it is a policy of control that stifles rather than promotes economic growth (Hweshe 2013). The by-law is seen as focusing on regulation rather than empowerment, as promoted in the Economic Growth Strategy. In this respect, it echoes the highly controversial Licensing of Businesses Bill that was withdrawn by national government following a chorus of protest from municipalities, big business, researchers and NGOs (Rogerson 2015).

The City of Cape Town's Single Zoning Scheme, also passed in 2013, has been criticized for acting in conjunction with the Informal Trading By-Law to further repress the informal sector. The scheme requires *spaza* shops to operate on Mondays to Saturdays from 7am to 9pm and from 8am to 1pm on Sundays and public holidays, and requires a separate structure for trading and that no area used for trading should open into a bedroom or toilet. This effectively renders 70% of *spaza* stores in Cape Town illegal (Western Cape Informal Traders Coalition et al 2013). The Western Cape Informal Traders Coalition, Somali Association of South Africa, Cosatu Western Cape, PASSOP, National Consumer Forum, South African Council of Churches, Scalabrini Foundation and the Legal Resources Centre have all questioned the rationale behind the new by-law and zoning scheme:

> The question may be asked whether these By-Laws were designed to benefit the Corporate Retailers who are increasingly encroaching on the townships with the proliferation of shopping malls. Are these unrealistic and unjustifiable requirements placed on spaza shops a disguised attempt to eliminate competition for Big Business especially Corporate Retailers, who are the stated preferred constituency of the political party ruling the City at the moment (Western Cape Informal Traders Coalition et al 2013).

8. POLICY RECOMMENDATIONS

The informal food retail sector is an important component of the food system and serves the needs of the urban poor. As this report has demonstrated, the sector is highly diverse, both in terms of the products traded and the business models utilized. The informal food retail sector does not exist independently of the formal food retail sector and intersects at various points upstream and through customer practices. It is therefore essential to view the formal and informal food sectors as part of the same food system and to generate policy and planning responses that acknowledge the role of both in meeting local food security needs. A number of policy and programme recommendations follow from this conclusion as well as the findings of this research.

8.1 Reduction of Food Spoilage

Many informal food vendors identified food spoilage as a critical problem. Given the marginal status of many of these businesses, any loss due to spoilage has a significant impact on business viability. Spoilage is the result both of poor storage and lack of refrigeration on site, and damage to products through cold chain lapses during transportation. It is therefore necessary to develop innovative solutions to reduce food spoilage, and to find safe means of disposal/recycling of waste.

8.2 Incentivization of Sale of Healthier Foods

The informal food retail sector is a frequent source of food for the urban poor. However, there are concerns about the nutritional quality of the available food. Much of the food sold by many *spaza* shops is highly processed because it stores well and is in demand. *Spaza* shops near schools generate much of their income through selling sweets, soft drinks and chips to children. Additionally, there is considerable food trade around transport hubs, such as train stations, but this food is often calorie-dense and nutritionally-deficient. Given the importance of sites such as train stations and areas around schools as sources of pre-prepared foods, there is an opportunity for the City to incentivize the retail of healthier foods in these sites.

The experiences of the Green Carts and Shop Healthy projects in New York City provide insights into the possibilities and challenges associated with such initiatives (Bansal 2012, Jahn and Shavitz 2012). Strategies to increase entrepreneurialism in the informal sector do not necessarily have positive outcomes for food and nutrition security. Within informal food retail, it makes better economic sense to trade in highly processed, less healthy foods. There is therefore a need for targeted interventions to promote the sale and consumption of healthier foods.

8.3 Balancing Regulation with Support for Food Vendors

There are concerns that the current approach to informal trade in the City is too focused on regulation and insufficiently supportive of informal vendors, despite statements by the City to the contrary (Bloor 2013).

There are legitimate concerns that the new Informal Trading By-Law places unreasonable conditions on informal traders, thus undermining its stated intention of enhancing informal trade. This imbalance between regulation and support is particularly evident in the informal food retail sector, where public health concerns often lead to a stronger regulatory response. There has certainly been longstanding concern about the street trade of meat and informal abattoirs. In 2008, for example, the former head of the municipal Maitland Abattoir said that the informal abattoirs were a health hazard and should be closed down, noting that sickly and low-quality stock are sold into the informal system. At the time, it was suggested that the rise in informal abattoirs was the result of the closure of the abattoir in Maitland. The head of the City's Health Department called for an accommodating approach that involved education and technical support (Bamford 2008). This issue was raised again in 2014, with the SPCA arguing that the informal meat sector was breaking the Animals Protection Act and the Meat Safety Act, as well as various health and environmental by-laws. In response, the City indicated that, together with the provincial Department of Agriculture, it is conducting a feasibility study on mobile abattoirs. However, by mid-2016 the study had still not been released.

8.4 Recognition of the Role of Informal Food Businesses in Food Security Policy

In policy documents, the informal sector is framed almost entirely as a source of employment and potential entrepreneurialism. While this is important, it is also necessary for informal sector policy to recognize the role that food businesses play in the food system that delivers food to the urban poor. The City needs to recognize the informal sector for the services it offers, including food security, and not just its role as a source of employment. Through a better understanding of the geography and economics of how this sector meets the food security needs of the urban poor, it should be possible to refine policies, programmes and by-laws to enhance the sector.

8.5 Integrated Food System Planning

By viewing the informal food retail sector as part of the wider food system, it is possible to connect policies and planning regarding formal and informal retail and other components of the food system. There is an obvious need for integrated food system planning. At present, there is little explicit food system planning within South Africa at national, provincial or municipal government levels. Food security projects are generally responding to problems within the food system, rather than seeking to obviate them. There is a need for more analysis of the food system and the assumptions and biases that drive its structure. At the municipal level there is a need for greater awareness of the activities conducted within the existing mandates that shape the food system, including spatial planning, zoning regulations, transport planning, and environmental health regulation.

If the constitutional right to food is to be achieved, it will be necessary to develop a multi-departmental food system and food security strategy that champions and facilitates the progressive realization of the right of all residents to access sufficient, nutritious, safe and culturally appropriate food. This should involve strategic interventions into the existing food system and the planning of new food system components that will enable households to meet their food needs. This report argues that the informal food retail sector is a vital component of any food system. The informal food retail sector provides essential food for the urban poor and it is vital that the sector be supported by the City.

REFERENCES

1. Bamford, H. (2008). "'Slabattoirs' are Health Time-Bombs" *IOL* 16 February.
2. Bamu, P. and Theron , J. (2012). "Nothing About Us Without Us: A Case Study of the Dynamics of the Informal Workplace at Mitchell's Plain Town Centre" Development and Labour Monograph Series No. 01/2012, Faculty of Law, University of Cape Town.
3. Bansal, S. (2012) "The Healthy Bodegas Initiative: Bringing Good Food to the Desert" *The Atlantic* 3 April.
4. Basadien, F., Parker, H., Bayat, M., Friedrich, C. and Appoles, S. (2014). "Entrepreneurial Orientation of Spaza Shop Entrepreneurs: Evidence from a Study of South African and Somali Owned Spaza Entrepreneurs in Khayelitsha" *Singapore Journal of Business Economics and Management Studies* 2: 45-61.
5. Battersby, J. (2011a). *The State of Urban Food Security in Cape Town*, Urban Food Security Series No. 11, AFSUN, Cape Town.
6. Battersby, J. (2011b). "Urban Food Insecurity in Cape Town, South Africa: An Alternative Approach to Food Access" *Development Southern Africa* 28: 545-561.
7. Battersby, J. (2012). "Beyond the Food Desert: Finding Ways to Speak about Urban Food Security in South Africa" *Geographiska Annaler* 94: 141-58.
8. Battersby, J. and Peyton, S. (2014). "The Geography of Supermarkets in Cape Town: Supermarket Expansion and Food Access" *Urban Forum* 25: 153-164.
9. Bear, M., Bradnum, P., Tladi, S. and Pedro, D. (2005). "Making Retail Markets Work for the Poor: Why and How Triple Trust Organisation Decided to Intervene in the Spaza Market in South Africa" SEEP Network, Washington DC.

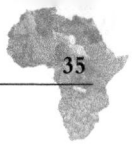

10. Bisseker, C. (2006). "Retailers' Drive into the Township Market Threatens Spaza Shops" *Business Day* 28 September.

11. Bloor, G. (2013). "Cape Town: An Opportunity City" *Business Day* 30 October.

12. Charman, A., Petersen, L. and Piper, L. (2012). "From Local Survivalism to Foreign Entrepreneurship: The Transformation of the Spaza Sector in Delft, Cape Town" *Transformation* 78: 47-73.

13. CoCT (2003). "Informal Trading Policy and Management Framework" City of Cape Town, Cape Town, South Africa.

14. CoCT (2013a). *Economic Growth Strategy*. City of Cape Town, Cape Town.

15. CoCT (2013b) *Draft Social Development Strategy: Informal Trading*. City of Cape Town, Cape Town.

16. Coetzer, P. and Pascarel, N. (2014). "Last Mile Delivery in Low Income Communities: The Sekulula Spaza Express Experiment in South Africa" *Field Actions Science Reports* Special Issue 12.

17. Coates J.; Swindale, A. and Bilinsky, P. (2007). *Household Food Insecurity Access Scale (HFIAS) for Measurement of Household Food Access: Indicator Guide*. Washington, DC: FANTA.

18. Competition Commission (2008). "Competition Commission Focus on Agriculture and Food Value Chains" *Competition News* 29: 1-4.

19. Cooke, K. (2012). "Urban Food Access: A Study of the Lived Experience of Food Access within a Low Income Community in Cape Town" MA Thesis, University of Cape Town, Cape Town.

20. Crush, J. and Frayne, B. (2011). "Supermarket Expansion and the Informal Food Economy in Southern African Cities: Implications for Urban Food Security" *Journal of Southern African Studies* 37: 781-807.

21. DAFF (2012). "Agro-Processing Strategy" Department of Agriculture, Forestry and Fisheries, Pretoria.

22. DAFF (2014). *The National Policy on Food and Nutrition Security for the Republic of South Africa*. Government Gazette No. 637, Pretoria, 22 August.

23. Dano, Z. (2014). "'Slabattoirs' Should Get the Chop: SPCA" *IOL* 21 July.

24. D'Haese, M. and Van Huylenbroech, G. (2005). "The Rise of Supermarkets and Changing Expenditure Patterns of Poor Rural Households: Case Study in the Transkei area, South Africa" *Food Policy* 30: 97-113.

25. DoA (2002). *Integrated Food Security Strategy for South Africa*. Pretoria: Department of Agriculture.

26. DoH (2002). *Integrated Nutrition Plan: Strategic Plan 2002/2003 to 2006/2007*. Pretoria: Department of Health.

27. Dolan, D. (2014). "South African 'Spaza' Shops Suffer as Big Retail Rolls In" *Reuters* 20 April.

28. Drimie, S. and Ruysenaar, S. (2010)." The Integrated Food Security Strategy of South Africa: An Institutional Analysis" *Agrekon* 49: 326-337.

29. DTI (2011). *Industrial Policy Action Plan (IPAP2) 2011/12-2013/14*. Pretoria: Department of Trade and Industry.

30. Economist (2014). "Somali Shop-Swap" *The Economist* 22 March.

31. FPMC (2003). "Food Price Monitoring Committee Final Report" Department of Agriculture, Forestries and Fisheries, Pretoria.

32. GAIN (2012). "Republic of South Africa. Retail Food Sector Grows Despite Downturn" Global Agricultural Information Network, USDA, Washington DC.

33. Gastrow, V. and Amit, R. (2015). "The Role of Migrant Traders in Local Economies: A Case Study of Somali Spaza Shops in Cape Town" In J. Crush, A. Chikanda and C. Skinner, eds., *Mean Streets: Migration, Xenophobia and Informality in South Africa*. Ottawa: IDRC, pp. 162-177.

34. Greenberg, S. (2010). "Contesting the Food System in South Africa: Issues and Opportunities" PLAAS Research Report No. 42, University of the Western Cape, Cape Town.

35. Humphrey, J. (2007). "The Supermarket Revolution in Developing Countries: Tidal Wave or Tough Competitive Struggle?" *Journal of Economic Geography* 7: 433-50.

36. Hweshe, F. (2013), "Report Criticizes City's Informal Trading Bylaws" *West Cape News* 26 March.

37. Igumbor, E., Sanders, D., Puoane, T., Tsolekile, L., Schwarz, C., Purdy, C., Swart, R., Durão, S. and Hawkes, C. (2012). "'Big Food,' the Consumer Food Environment, Health, and the Policy Response in South Africa" *PLoS Medicine* 9(7).

38. Jackson, A. (2010). "The Complex Food System: A Case Study of Soft Vegetables Produced in the Philippi Horticultural Area and the Soft Vegetables Sold by Traders Purchased at Different Links in the Food System" MPhil Thesis, University of Cape Town, Cape Town.

39. Jahn, M. and Shavitz, M. (2012). "Green Cart Vendors Face Diet of Challenges" *citylimits.org* 9 January.

40. Kelly, P. (2013). "Revised 'Basket' Makes CPI More Accurate and Relevant" *Business Day* 19 February.

41. Labadarios, D., Steyn, N., Maunder, M., MacIntryre, U., Gericke, G., Swart, R., Huskisson, J., Dannhauser, A., Vorster, H., Nesamvuni, A. and Nel, J. (2005). "The National Food Consumption Survey (NFCS): South Africa, 1999" *Public Health Nutrition* 8: 533-543.

42. Ligthelm, A. (2008). "The Impact of Shopping Mall Developments on Small Township Retailers" *South African Journal of Economic and Management Sciences* NS 11: 37-53.

43. Madlokazi, N. (2011). "An Analysis of Solid Waste Generation and Management by Informal Meat Traders, Khayelitsha, Cape Town" MPhil Thesis, University of Cape Town, Cape Town.

44. Magwaza, N. (2013). "Pick n Pay to Face Off with Shoprite" *IOL* 12 April.

45. Mantshantsha, S. (2013). "BP Teams Up with Pick n Pay in Retail Deal" *Business Day* 24 April.

46. McGaffin, R. (2010). "Shopping Centres in Township Areas: Blessing or Curse?" Report for Urban Landmark, Pretoria.

47. Moneyweb (2013). "Shoprite FY Profit up 11.3%" *Moneyweb* 20 August.

48. Nagdee. Q. (2004). "The Debt Trap: The Indebtedness of the Poor in South Africa" MA Thesis, Institute of Social Development, University of the Western Cape, Cape Town.

49. NPC (2012). *National Development Plan. Vision for 2030*. Pretoria: National Planning Commission.

50.   Peyton, S., Moseley, W. and Battersby, J. (2015). "Implications of Supermarket Expansion on Urban Food Security in Cape Town, South Africa" *African Geographical Review* 34: 36-54.

51.   Pienaar, R. (2011). "Pick n Pay Food Security" Sustainable Food Lab, Cape Town.

52.   Planting, S. (2010). "Into the Trolley" *Financial Mail* 23 July.

53.   Preisendörfer, P., Bitz, A. and Bezuidenhout, F. (2012). "Business Start-Ups and Their Prospects of Success in South African Townships" *South African Review of Sociology* 43: 3-23.

54.   Ramabulana, T. (2011). "The Rise of South African Agribusiness: The Good, The Bad, and the Ugly" *Agrekon* 50: 102-109.

55.   Reardon, T. and Timmer, C. (2012). "The Economics of the Food System Revolution" *Annual Review of Resource Economics* 4: 225-64.

56.   Reardon, T., Henson, S. and Berdegúe, J. (2007). "'Proactive Fast-Tracking' Diffusion of Supermarkets in Developing Countries: Implications for Markets, Institutions and Trade" *Journal of Economic Geography* 7: 399-431.

57.   Reardon, T. and Minten, B. (2011). "The Quiet Revolution in India's Food Supply Chains" IFPRI Discussion Paper 01115, Washington DC.

58.   Rogan, M. and Skinner, C. (2017). "Employment in the South African Informal Sector: Interrogating Trends, Identifying Opportunities" In F. Fourie, ed., *Tackling Unemployment and Poverty in South Africa: The Contribution of the Informal Sector.* Cape Town: HSRC.

59.   Rogerson, C. (2016). "South Africa's Informal Economy: Reframing Debates in National Policy" *Local Economy* 31: 172-186.

60.   Section 27 (2015). "Call for Wider Policy Consultation" Johannesburg.

61.   Skinner, C. (2008). "The Struggle for the Streets: Processes of Exclusion and Inclusion of Street Traders in Durban, South Africa" *Development Southern Africa* 25: 227-242.

62.   Skinner, C. and Haysom, G. (2016). "The Informal Sector's Role in Food Security: A Missing Link in Policy Debates?" Working Paper No. 44, PLAAS, UWC and Centre of Excellence on Food Security, Cape Town.

63.   StatsSA (2012). "Quarterly Labour Force Survey, Quarter 4, 2012" Statistics South Africa, Pretoria.

64.   Strydom, J. (2011). "Retailing in Disadvantaged Communities: The Outshopping Phenomenon Revisited" *Journal of Contemporary Management* 8: 150-172.

65.   Traill, W. (2006). "The Rapid Rise of Supermarkets?" *Development Policy Review* 24: 163-74.

66.   Tustin, D. and Strydom, J. (2006). "The Potential Impacts of the Formal Retail Chains' Expansion Strategies on Retail Township Development in South Africa" *South African Business Review* 10: 48-66.

67.   Van der Heijden, T. and Vink, N. (2013). "Good for Whom? Supermarkets and Small Farmers in South Africa: A Critical Review of Current Approaches to Increasing Access to Modern Markets" *Agrekon* 52: 68-86.

68.   Vink, N. and Kirsten, J. (2002). "Pricing Behaviour in the South African Food and Agricultural Sector" Report to the National Treasury, Pretoria.

69.   Vink, N. and Van Rooyen, J. (2009). "The Economic Performance of Agriculture

in South Africa since 1994: Implications for Food Security" Development Planning Division Working Paper Series No.17, Development Bank of Southern Africa, Midrand.

70. Weatherspoon, D. and Reardon, T. (2003). "The Rise of Supermarkets in Africa: Implications for Agrifood Systems and the Rural Poor" *Development Policy Review* 21: 333-55.

71. Western Cape Informal Traders Coalition, Somali Association of South Africa, Cosatu Western Cape, Passop, National Consumer Forum, South African Council of Churches, Scalabrini Foundation and Legal Resources Centre (2013). "Cape Town Zoning Schemes and By-Laws Challenged in the Informal Sector" at http://www.streetnet.org.za/show.php?id=491

72. Woodward, D., Rolfe, R., Ligthelm, A. and Guimarães, P. (2011). "The Viability of Informal Micro-Enterprise in South Africa" *Journal of Developmental Entrepreneurship* 16: 65-86.

73. Zager, K. (2011). "Commutes, Constraints, and Food: The Geography of Choice" BA Honours Thesis, University of Cape Town, Cape Town.

www.ingramcontent.com/pod-product-compliance
Lightning Source LLC
Chambersburg PA
CBHW080556270326
41929CB00019B/3329